# AI Portfolio Management & Scaling

## How to Use AI to Manage Properties, Automate Operations, and Scale Faster

*By Joe Correa*

AF850692

Published by Live Stronger Faster

Copyright © 2026 by Joe Correa

All rights reserved.

No part of this publication may be reproduced, distributed, or transmitted in any form or by any means—electronic, mechanical, photocopying, recording, or otherwise—without the prior written permission of the publisher, except in the case of brief quotations embodied in critical reviews and certain other noncommercial uses permitted by copyright law.

This book is for educational and informational purposes only. The author and publisher are not engaged in rendering legal, financial, or other professional advice. Readers should consult a qualified professional before making any financial decisions.

First Edition

# Table of Contents

# Introduction

In today's real estate landscape, the difference between a small portfolio and a truly scalable, wealth-generating real estate empire is no longer just capital, location, or even experience. The real differentiator has become systems. Specifically, intelligent systems powered by artificial intelligence that remove inefficiencies, reduce manual decision-making, and allow investors to operate at a level of speed and precision that was previously impossible. This is the foundation of Book 9: AI Portfolio Management & Scaling. At this stage of the series, you are no longer simply learning how to find deals, analyze properties, or finance investments. You are now stepping into the role of portfolio operator—someone who must oversee multiple assets, multiple income streams, and multiple moving parts simultaneously while maintaining profitability, efficiency, and long-term growth. This requires a shift in mindset from reactive investing to proactive system design. AI becomes the bridge between owning properties and truly scaling them into a structured, automated, and optimized business.

As your portfolio grows, so does complexity. What once was manageable with spreadsheets and manual oversight quickly becomes overwhelming when you are tracking dozens of tenants, maintenance requests, income streams, loan payments, property taxes, insurance renewals, vacancies, and capital expenditures. Without automation, investors often hit a ceiling—not because they cannot acquire more properties, but because they cannot manage them efficiently. This is where AI-driven portfolio management becomes essential. Instead of reacting to problems after they occur, AI systems allow investors to predict issues before they happen, optimize performance in real time, and centralize decision-making into intelligent dashboards. Platforms such as Buildium and AppFolio are examples of how modern property management has evolved into fully integrated ecosystems that handle everything from rent collection and accounting to maintenance coordination and tenant communication. When combined with AI-enhanced workflows, these platforms become more than tools—they become operational command centers for real estate businesses.

The true power of AI in portfolio management lies in its ability to unify fragmented systems into one intelligent structure. Traditionally, real estate investors rely on separate tools for accounting, property management, tenant screening, maintenance tracking, and financial forecasting. Each system operates independently, requiring manual reconciliation and oversight. AI changes this by connecting data points across all properties and turning them into actionable insights. Instead of looking at each property individually, AI allows you to view your entire portfolio as a living, dynamic system that continuously optimizes itself. For example, AI can analyze rent trends across neighborhoods, compare them to your current lease structures, and recommend rent adjustments that maximize cash flow without increasing vacancy risk. It can identify which properties are underperforming, not just in terms of income, but also in terms of maintenance costs, tenant turnover, or long-term appreciation potential.

This level of intelligence transforms how investors think about scaling. Scaling is no longer just about acquiring more properties; it is about building a system that can absorb growth without breaking. Many investors make the mistake of expanding too quickly without infrastructure, leading to operational chaos. Missed maintenance requests, delayed rent collection, poor tenant communication, and financial blind spots become common. AI prevents this breakdown by introducing structure at scale. It ensures that every property is monitored, every financial transaction is tracked, and every operational task is prioritized based on urgency and impact. This allows investors to grow portfolios with confidence, knowing that the system supporting them is designed to handle expansion.

Another critical component of AI portfolio management is predictive maintenance. One of the most expensive and unpredictable aspects of real estate investing is maintenance and repairs. Traditionally, issues are addressed only after they become visible problems, often resulting in higher costs and tenant dissatisfaction. AI changes this reactive model into a predictive one. By analyzing historical maintenance data, seasonal patterns, property age, and usage behavior, AI systems can forecast when systems are likely to fail. For example, HVAC systems, plumbing issues, roof deterioration, and appliance failures can all be predicted with increasing accuracy. This allows investors to schedule maintenance proactively, reduce emergency repair costs, and extend the lifespan of property assets. Over time, this creates significant savings and increases net operating income across the portfolio.

Financial tracking and optimization are also fundamentally transformed through AI. Instead of reviewing monthly statements and manually calculating performance metrics, AI continuously evaluates cash flow, debt service coverage ratios, return on equity, and internal rate of return across all assets. It can identify which properties are contributing most to portfolio growth and which ones are stagnating or underperforming. More importantly, AI can recommend strategic actions such as refinancing opportunities, selling underperforming assets, or reallocating capital toward higher-yield investments. This turns portfolio management into an active, data-driven process rather than a passive review of historical performance. Investors are no longer guessing—they are making decisions based on real-time intelligence.

Scaling is also deeply tied to operational efficiency, particularly in tenant management and communication. One of the biggest challenges in managing multiple properties is maintaining consistent, timely communication with tenants while ensuring high satisfaction and low turnover. AI-powered automation solves this by handling routine communication tasks such as rent reminders, lease renewals, maintenance updates, and inquiry responses. This not only reduces workload but also improves tenant experience by ensuring faster response times and consistent communication. Over time, this leads to higher retention rates, fewer vacancies, and more stable cash flow. AI can even analyze tenant behavior patterns to identify potential risks, such as late payment trends or maintenance complaints, allowing investors to intervene before issues escalate.

Another important dimension of AI portfolio scaling is data centralization. Real estate investors often struggle with fragmented information spread across emails, spreadsheets, bank accounts, property management systems, and third-party platforms. AI solves this by aggregating all relevant data into unified dashboards that provide real-time visibility into portfolio performance. This centralized intelligence allows investors to make faster and more informed decisions. Instead of spending hours gathering data, investors can instantly see key performance indicators across their entire portfolio. This shift in efficiency alone can dramatically increase scalability, as decision-making becomes faster, more accurate, and less dependent on manual analysis.

As portfolios grow, strategic expansion becomes increasingly important. AI plays a critical role in identifying where and how to scale next. By analyzing market trends, demographic shifts, rental demand, job growth, and property appreciation patterns, AI can highlight emerging investment opportunities before they become widely recognized. This gives investors a significant competitive advantage, allowing them to enter markets early and acquire assets at favorable prices. Additionally, AI can simulate different expansion scenarios, helping investors understand the financial impact of adding new properties under different financing structures or market conditions. This turns scaling into a calculated, strategic process rather than a speculative one.

Risk management is another area where AI fundamentally changes portfolio operations. Every real estate portfolio carries risk—market fluctuations, interest rate changes, tenant defaults, regulatory shifts, and unexpected maintenance costs. AI continuously monitors these variables and provides early warning signals when risk levels increase. For example, if interest rates rise and begin affecting cash flow on variable loans, AI can alert the investor and recommend refinancing strategies. If a specific market shows declining rental demand, AI can suggest divestment or repositioning strategies. This proactive risk management ensures that portfolios remain resilient even in changing economic conditions.

Ultimately, AI portfolio management is about freedom. It is about creating systems that allow investors to step away from day-to-day operations without sacrificing performance. It is about building a business that runs intelligently, adapts automatically, and scales sustainably. When implemented correctly, AI does not just improve efficiency—it transforms real estate investing into a highly optimized, semi-autonomous wealth-building machine. Investors are no longer trapped in operational details; instead, they become strategic architects of a system that works continuously on their behalf.

As you move through this book, you will begin to see real estate not as a collection of individual properties, but as an interconnected ecosystem. Each asset feeds into the next. Each decision impacts the whole. And each optimization compounds over time. AI becomes the intelligence layer that ties everything together, ensuring that nothing is overlooked and everything is optimized. The result is not just better property management—it is exponential portfolio growth. This is the next evolution of real estate investing. Not manual. Not reactive. Not fragmented. But intelligent, automated, and scalable. And once you understand how to build and deploy these systems effectively, you unlock the ability to grow your portfolio far beyond traditional limits.

Chapter 1

# The New Era Of Ai Portfolio Intelligence

The moment an investor moves beyond a single property, everything changes. The game is no longer about finding one good deal, negotiating one strong purchase, or analyzing one rental property. It becomes about managing a system of assets that must all perform together in harmony. This is where most investors begin to feel the weight of scale—not because real estate stops being profitable, but because the complexity begins to outpace their ability to manage it manually. Chapter 1 introduces the foundation of AI Portfolio Management & Scaling: understanding that real estate success at scale is no longer defined by how many properties you own, but by how intelligently those properties are managed, optimized, and interconnected through systems powered by artificial intelligence.

At its core, AI portfolio intelligence is about replacing fragmentation with integration. Traditional real estate investors operate in silos. One spreadsheet tracks income, another tracks expenses, a separate system handles tenants, another handles maintenance requests, and bank accounts sit disconnected from operational data. As the portfolio grows, these disconnected systems become a bottleneck. Mistakes multiply. Opportunities are missed. Cash flow becomes harder to predict. AI changes this structure entirely by consolidating all of these data points into a unified intelligence layer. Instead of manually analyzing performance, investors begin to operate from a real-time command center where decisions are informed instantly by data.

This shift is not just technological—it is philosophical. It requires investors to stop thinking like property owners and start thinking like system designers. A property is no longer an isolated investment; it is a node within a larger portfolio ecosystem. That ecosystem is constantly producing data—rents collected, expenses incurred, tenant behavior patterns, maintenance cycles, market fluctuations—and AI becomes the engine that interprets this data continuously. The investor's role evolves from managing tasks to managing strategy. Instead of reacting to problems, they begin to anticipate them before they occur.

One of the most important components of AI portfolio intelligence is automation of financial oversight. In traditional investing, financial performance is reviewed monthly or quarterly. By the time issues are identified, damage may already be done. AI eliminates this delay by tracking financial performance in real time. Cash flow is no longer a static number on a spreadsheet—it becomes a dynamic metric that updates continuously as rent is collected, expenses are processed, and loan payments are made. This allows investors to see immediately when a property is underperforming or when a portfolio is deviating from its expected trajectory.

Another key transformation is the way AI handles operational management. Property management is often the most time-consuming aspect of scaling real estate. Tenant communication, maintenance coordination, lease renewals, rent collection, and vendor management all require constant attention. Platforms such as Buildium and AppFolio have already introduced automation into these workflows, but AI takes this a step further by adding predictive intelligence. Instead of simply managing tasks, AI begins to prioritize them based on urgency, cost impact, and long-term portfolio performance.

For example, a traditional system might notify a landlord that a maintenance request has been submitted. An AI-powered system, however, can analyze the request in context. It can determine whether this issue is isolated or part of a recurring pattern across multiple properties. It can estimate the potential cost if the issue is delayed. It can even recommend the optimal vendor based on past performance, pricing, and response time. This transforms property management from reactive coordination into proactive optimization. As portfolios grow, one of the most critical challenges investors face is decision fatigue. With multiple properties, multiple markets, and multiple financial variables, it becomes increasingly difficult to determine where attention should be focused. AI solves this by introducing prioritization intelligence. Instead of overwhelming the investor with data, it highlights what actually matters. Which property is underperforming relative to market benchmarks. Which tenants are at risk of late payment. Which expenses are trending upward. Which properties are approaching refinance or sale optimization windows. This allows investors to focus their energy where it has the highest impact on portfolio growth.

Another major advantage of AI portfolio management is its ability to create predictive financial models. Traditional investors rely on historical data to make future decisions. AI, however, can simulate multiple future scenarios based on changing variables such as interest rates, rental demand, vacancy trends, and property appreciation. This allows investors to understand not just what their portfolio is doing now, but what it is likely to do under different economic conditions. This predictive capability transforms risk management from reactive defense into proactive strategy.

Scaling, in this new environment, becomes a function of system readiness rather than emotional confidence. Many investors hesitate to grow because they fear losing control. They worry that more properties will mean more stress, more complexity, and more mistakes. AI eliminates this barrier by ensuring that systems scale automatically alongside portfolio growth. Whether an investor owns five properties or fifty, the system remains structured, organized, and optimized. Every new property is absorbed into the existing framework without increasing operational chaos.

This introduces a fundamental shift in mindset: growth is no longer limited by management capacity. Instead, growth becomes limited only by acquisition opportunity and capital access. If the system can manage it, the investor can own it. This is the true power of AI portfolio intelligence—it removes the traditional ceiling on real estate scaling.

The final layer of this transformation is strategic insight. AI does not just manage operations; it begins to reveal patterns that would otherwise remain invisible. It can identify which types of properties consistently outperform others. It can detect which neighborhoods are entering growth cycles. It can highlight inefficiencies in financing structures across the portfolio. Over time, this creates a feedback loop where every decision improves the next one. The portfolio becomes smarter as it grows. Ultimately, Chapter 1 establishes the foundation for everything that follows. AI portfolio management is not just a toolset—it is a new operating system for real estate investing. It replaces fragmentation with integration, manual oversight with automation, and reactive management with predictive intelligence. Investors who adopt this system early gain a compounding advantage that becomes increasingly difficult for traditional investors to match.

This is where real estate investing evolves from ownership to orchestration. From managing properties to managing intelligence. From working in the business to designing the system that runs the business.

And once that shift is made, scale is no longer something you chase—it becomes something that happens naturally.

### *The Investor Who Stopped Managing And Started Building Systems*

Daniel had always believed that real estate success came down to effort. He prided himself on being hands-on, detailed, and involved in every part of his portfolio. At first, it worked. With one duplex, then a small four-unit building, he could stay on top of everything. Rent collection was simple. Maintenance was manageable. Financial tracking lived in a spreadsheet he updated every Sunday night. He felt in control.

But control slowly began to slip away as he acquired more properties. By the time Daniel reached twelve doors, his weekends disappeared. He was constantly responding to tenant messages, coordinating repairs, reviewing expenses, and trying to reconcile bank statements with his spreadsheets. At twenty doors, things became chaotic. He missed a rent increase opportunity in one unit because he was too busy dealing with a plumbing issue in another. He overlooked a recurring maintenance pattern in three different properties that later cost him thousands in emergency repairs.

The breaking point came one evening when he realized he had spent nearly four hours trying to figure out why one property's cash flow report did not match his expectations. The answer, when he finally found it, was simple: a series of small overlooked expenses that had quietly accumulated over months. There was no single catastrophic mistake—just fragmentation. Too many systems. Too many details. Too many blind spots.

That night, Daniel almost decided to slow down his investing. He thought maybe he had reached his limit.

Instead, something unexpected happened. A fellow investor introduced him to a new way of thinking—not about working harder, but about building systems that worked without him.

At first, Daniel was skeptical. He had used property management software before, but it still required constant input and oversight. But this was different. He was introduced to platforms like Buildium and AppFolio not just as tools for organization, but as foundations for automation. More importantly, he was introduced to the idea that artificial intelligence could sit on top of these systems and make them intelligent.

Daniel began slowly. He did not change everything at once. Instead, he started by integrating his properties into a unified system. Instead of separate spreadsheets, everything flowed into one dashboard. Instead of manually tracking maintenance, requests were centralized. Instead of guessing financial performance, he saw real-time updates.

The first real change he noticed was not financial—it was mental. The constant pressure disappeared. He no longer felt like he was chasing problems. He began to see patterns instead of chaos. He could finally breathe.

Then the system started doing something he did not expect.

It began to tell him things he did not know.

One of his properties had been slowly increasing in maintenance costs over time. Another had tenants with consistently longer retention rates. One neighborhood was showing stronger rent growth than others in his portfolio.

These were not things he had actively tracked before. They were insights revealed through aggregation and analysis.

For the first time, Daniel was not reacting to problems—he was seeing opportunities.

Six months later, everything had changed.

His portfolio had grown, but his workload had not. In fact, he was working less than before. The system handled tenant communication. It flagged maintenance issues before they became expensive. It tracked financial performance in real time. And most importantly, it gave him clarity instead of confusion.

One evening, Daniel sat back and realized something powerful: he was no longer managing properties. He was managing a system that managed properties for him.

That was the moment everything shifted.

He stopped thinking like a landlord.

He started thinking like an architect of systems.

And from that point forward, his growth no longer felt like pressure. It felt like momentum.

*Chapter 2*

# Centralized Intelligence And Real-Time Portfolio Control

As real estate portfolios expand, one of the most important challenges investors face is not acquisition, financing, or even tenant management—it is visibility. The more properties an investor owns, the harder it becomes to see the full picture clearly. Data becomes scattered across platforms, decisions become delayed, and performance becomes reactive rather than strategic. Chapter 2 introduces the next evolution in AI Portfolio Management & Scaling: centralized intelligence. This is the concept of bringing every moving part of a real estate portfolio into one unified, real-time system where data is not only collected but actively interpreted, analyzed, and transformed into actionable decisions.

Centralized intelligence begins with a simple but powerful idea: no piece of information in a real estate portfolio should exist in isolation. Every rent payment, maintenance request, expense, lease renewal, vacancy, and loan obligation is connected. Traditionally, investors are forced to manually connect these dots themselves, often long after the events have already impacted performance. AI removes this delay by acting as the central nervous system of the portfolio. Instead of information flowing to the investor for interpretation, the system itself interprets it continuously and presents only what matters most in real time.

At the core of this system are property management platforms like Buildium and AppFolio, which serve as the operational backbone for centralized portfolio management. These platforms consolidate tenant data, financial records, maintenance tracking, and communication history into a single ecosystem. However, when layered with artificial intelligence, they evolve from administrative tools into intelligent decision-making engines. AI does not just store data—it evaluates it, compares it, predicts outcomes, and recommends actions based on portfolio-wide performance trends.

One of the most powerful transformations enabled by centralized intelligence is real-time financial awareness. In traditional investing, financial reports are backward-looking. Investors review monthly statements and attempt to understand what already happened. By the time inefficiencies are identified, they have often already compounded into significant losses. AI replaces this lag with continuous financial monitoring. Cash flow is no longer a static snapshot—it becomes a live metric that updates instantly as transactions occur. This allows investors to see performance as it happens, not after the fact. This real-time visibility fundamentally changes decision-making. Instead of asking, "How did my portfolio perform last month?" investors begin asking, "What is happening in my portfolio right now, and what should I do about it immediately?" This shift enables faster responses to problems and quicker capitalization on opportunities. For example, if a property begins trending toward negative cash flow due to rising expenses, AI can flag the issue immediately, identify the cause, and suggest corrective action such as rent adjustment, expense reduction, or refinancing analysis.

Another key component of centralized intelligence is operational synchronization. In a fragmented system, different parts of the business operate independently. Leasing decisions are made without full awareness of maintenance costs. Maintenance decisions are made without considering financial impact. Tenant communications are handled separately from portfolio performance tracking. AI eliminates these silos by synchronizing all operations into one cohesive system. Every action is evaluated not just in isolation, but in terms of its impact on the entire portfolio.

This synchronization extends into tenant management as well. Instead of treating each property as a separate entity, AI evaluates tenant behavior patterns across the entire portfolio.

It can identify which tenant profiles are most stable, which lease structures result in longer retention, and which properties experience higher turnover rates. This allows investors to refine their leasing strategies over time, reducing vacancy rates and increasing long-term stability. Centralized intelligence turns tenant data into strategic insight rather than isolated records.

Maintenance management also becomes significantly more efficient under centralized intelligence. Traditionally, maintenance is one of the most unpredictable and costly aspects of property ownership. Issues are often addressed only after tenants report them, leading to reactive repairs and higher costs. AI changes this by identifying patterns across multiple properties. If similar issues begin occurring in different units or buildings, the system can detect early warning signals and recommend preventative action. This shifts maintenance from reactive repair to predictive management, reducing costs and improving asset longevity.

Another major advantage of centralized intelligence is portfolio-wide risk monitoring. Real estate risk is rarely isolated to a single property. Economic shifts, interest rate changes, insurance increases, and local market fluctuations can affect multiple assets simultaneously. Without centralized visibility, these risks often go unnoticed until they have already impacted performance. AI continuously monitors external and internal variables across the entire portfolio, identifying risk exposure before it becomes critical. It can highlight overleveraged properties, declining markets, or underperforming assets, allowing investors to rebalance their portfolios proactively.

Centralized intelligence also transforms how investors think about scaling. In traditional models, scaling introduces complexity. More properties mean more spreadsheets, more calls, more decisions, and more potential for error. With AI-driven centralization, scaling does not increase complexity—it simply increases data volume within the same structured system. Whether an investor owns ten properties or one hundred, the system remains consistent. Every new property is automatically integrated into the existing framework, analyzed in context, and managed through the same intelligent dashboard.

This consistency creates what can be described as "infinite scalability without operational overload." Investors are no longer limited by their ability to personally manage details. Instead, they are limited only by acquisition opportunity and capital. The system itself does not break under scale; it strengthens as more data improves its predictive accuracy.

Another critical feature of centralized intelligence is decision acceleration. In traditional real estate investing, decisions often take days or weeks because data must be gathered, verified, and analyzed manually. AI reduces this timeline dramatically by pre-analyzing data and presenting pre-qualified recommendations. Instead of spending hours evaluating whether to refinance a property, for example, investors can receive instant analysis showing potential savings, break-even points, and long-term financial impact. This allows decisions to be made faster and with greater confidence.

As centralized intelligence matures, it begins to function not just as a management system, but as a strategic advisor. It learns from historical portfolio behavior, adapts to investor preferences, and refines its recommendations over time. This creates a feedback loop where every decision improves the next one. The system becomes more accurate, more efficient, and more aligned with long-term portfolio goals as it processes more data.

Ultimately, Chapter 2 represents a shift from fragmented oversight to unified control. It is the difference between managing multiple properties and managing a single intelligent system that contains multiple properties. Centralized intelligence removes uncertainty, reduces inefficiency, and enhances clarity at every level of real estate investing. It transforms portfolios from collections of assets into fully integrated ecosystems that operate with precision and intelligence. This is where real estate investing begins to feel less like management and more like orchestration. Every property plays a role. Every data point has meaning. Every decision is informed by the system as a whole.

And once this level of visibility is achieved, scaling is no longer difficult—it becomes inevitable.

*The Moment Everything Became One System*

Marcus had always been proud of how organized his real estate business was. He used spreadsheets, folders, property management software, and even custom dashboards he had built over the years. On the surface, everything looked structured. He knew his properties, he tracked his income, and he stayed on top of maintenance issues. But beneath that surface, something was starting to break.

It began subtly. A missed rent increase here. A delayed maintenance response there. A financial report that didn't quite match expectations but took days to reconcile. None of it seemed serious on its own. But together, they created friction—small inefficiencies that slowly began to compound.

At first, Marcus thought he just needed to work harder. So he did. He added more tools. More spreadsheets. More reminders. More systems. But instead of becoming more organized, everything became more fragmented. Information was everywhere, but clarity was nowhere.

The breaking point came during tax season.

Marcus spent an entire weekend trying to reconcile his portfolio. Tenants were tracked in one system, expenses in another, and bank deposits in another. Nothing matched perfectly. He realized, with growing frustration, that he did not actually have a single view of his business. He had multiple incomplete views stitched together manually.

That was the moment he realized the truth: he was not running a system. He was managing chaos.

A few weeks later, Marcus was introduced to a different approach—centralized intelligence. At first, it sounded like just another software upgrade. But as he began exploring platforms like Buildium and AppFolio, he realized something deeper was happening. This was not about adding tools. It was about removing fragmentation.

He started the transition slowly. First, he consolidated all his properties into a single platform. Then he integrated financial tracking. Then tenant communication. For the first time, everything lived in one place.

The change was immediate—but not in the way he expected.

At first, Marcus felt overwhelmed by how much data was suddenly visible. But then something shifted. Instead of chasing information across systems, he began to see everything at once. Rent collection status, maintenance requests, cash flow performance, vacancy trends—it was all there, updated in real time.

Then the system started showing him things he had never seen before.

One property was consistently generating higher maintenance costs than others. Another had unusually strong tenant retention. A third was quietly underperforming due to small recurring expenses he had never grouped together. These patterns had always existed—but he had never had the visibility to see them.

For the first time, Marcus was not reacting to problems. He was understanding his portfolio.

Months passed, and the way he worked completely changed.

Instead of spending weekends fixing spreadsheets, he spent

hours reviewing insights. Instead of reacting to tenant issues individually, he saw patterns across properties. Instead of guessing financial performance, he saw real-time updates across his entire portfolio. One evening, Marcus sat in front of his dashboard and realized something profound: he was no longer managing properties separately. He was managing one unified system.

Everything was connected.

Everything was visible.

Everything was intelligent.

And for the first time in years, he felt in control—not because he was doing more work, but because he could finally see everything clearly.

That was the moment Marcus understood what scaling truly meant.

It was not about adding more properties.

It was about turning everything into one system.

*Chapter 3*

# Predictive Maintenance And Ai-Driven Asset Preservation

As real estate portfolios scale, one of the most underestimated forces affecting long-term profitability is not acquisition cost or financing structure—it is maintenance. Repairs, system failures, and property deterioration do not just impact expenses; they directly influence tenant satisfaction, vacancy rates, insurance costs, and long-term asset value. In traditional real estate investing, maintenance is reactive. Something breaks, a tenant reports it, and the owner responds. This cycle repeats endlessly, creating unpredictable costs and constant operational disruption. Chapter 3 introduces a fundamentally different approach: predictive maintenance powered by artificial intelligence, where issues are identified before they become problems and resolved before they impact performance.

Predictive maintenance begins with a shift in mindset. Instead of viewing maintenance as an unpredictable expense, AI treats it as a measurable, analyzable pattern. Every property generates data—appliance usage, HVAC cycles, plumbing stress, weather exposure, tenant behavior, and repair history. Individually, these data points may seem insignificant. But when aggregated across time and across multiple properties, they reveal powerful patterns. AI systems analyze these patterns to forecast when systems are likely to fail, allowing investors to intervene proactively rather than reactively.

Platforms such as Buildium and AppFolio serve as the operational foundation for capturing maintenance data at scale. Every service request, repair cost, and vendor interaction is logged into a centralized system. When enhanced with artificial intelligence, this historical data becomes predictive intelligence. Instead of simply recording that an HVAC system failed in July, AI begins to identify that similar systems across multiple properties tend to show early warning signs three to four months prior, especially under specific usage or weather conditions.

This transformation turns maintenance into a forward-looking discipline. For example, rather than waiting for a water heater to fail, AI can analyze temperature fluctuations, age of the unit, past repair frequency, and seasonal usage spikes to estimate failure probability. If risk crosses a certain threshold, the system can alert the investor and recommend preemptive replacement or servicing. This not only reduces emergency repair costs but also prevents tenant dissatisfaction and potential lease terminations caused by prolonged service interruptions. One of the most powerful benefits of predictive maintenance is cost stabilization. In traditional real estate portfolios, maintenance costs fluctuate unpredictably. One month may be low, while the next month may bring multiple emergency repairs that disrupt cash flow projections. This unpredictability makes financial planning difficult and increases perceived investment risk. AI smooths this volatility by converting irregular expenses into scheduled, planned interventions. Instead of reacting to breakdowns, investors can budget for maintenance cycles in advance, creating financial stability and more accurate forecasting.

Another critical advantage is asset lifespan extension. Most property systems—roofs, HVAC units, plumbing, appliances—depreciate over time. However, the rate of depreciation is not fixed; it is influenced by usage patterns, environmental conditions, and maintenance quality. AI systems can identify early signs of accelerated wear and recommend corrective action that extends the usable life of these assets. For example, minor HVAC inefficiencies that would normally go unnoticed can be corrected early, preventing major system failure and extending the lifespan by years. Over a large portfolio, these extensions translate into significant capital savings.

Predictive maintenance also plays a major role in tenant retention. Tenants rarely leave solely due to rent increases;

more often, they leave due to repeated inconveniences such as unresolved maintenance issues, slow response times, or recurring property problems. AI reduces these friction points by ensuring maintenance issues are addressed before they escalate. When tenants consistently experience well-maintained properties and fast resolution times, satisfaction increases, lease renewals improve, and vacancy rates decrease. This creates a compounding effect on portfolio stability.

The financial impact of predictive maintenance extends beyond direct repair savings. It also influences insurance risk, property valuation, and long-term appreciation. Well-maintained properties are less likely to experience catastrophic failures, reducing insurance claims and potentially lowering premiums over time. Additionally, properties with documented maintenance efficiency and lower historical repair frequency often appraise higher, as they present lower operational risk to future buyers or lenders. In this way, maintenance becomes not just an expense category, but a value creation strategy.

AI-driven maintenance systems also improve vendor management efficiency. Traditionally, property owners rely on a network of contractors, plumbers, electricians, and maintenance personnel, often selected based on availability rather than performance data. Over time, this leads to inconsistent service quality. AI changes this by tracking vendor performance across multiple metrics such as response time, cost efficiency, job completion quality, and repeat issue frequency. The system can then recommend the most reliable vendors for specific types of repairs, improving consistency and reducing long-term costs.

Another key innovation is clustering analysis. AI does not just analyze individual properties—it analyzes groups of properties to identify systemic issues. For example, if multiple properties built within a certain time period begin experiencing similar plumbing issues, the system can flag this as a structural or design-related risk. This allows investors to take portfolio-wide action rather than treating each issue in isolation. In some cases, this insight can even inform future acquisition decisions, helping investors avoid properties with hidden systemic risks.

Predictive maintenance also integrates directly with financial forecasting. Because maintenance costs are one of the largest variable expenses in real estate investing, improving accuracy in this area significantly enhances overall portfolio planning. Instead of estimating annual repair budgets based on historical averages, AI generates dynamic projections based on real-time property conditions. This allows investors to allocate capital more efficiently, maintain higher reserves when needed, and reduce unnecessary capital stagnation in low-risk periods. As portfolios scale, the importance of predictive maintenance increases exponentially. A single unexpected repair in a small portfolio may be manageable. However, in a large portfolio, multiple simultaneous failures can create financial strain and operational overload. AI reduces this risk by distributing maintenance events more evenly over time through early intervention. This creates a smoother operational curve, reducing stress on both financial and management systems.

Ultimately, predictive maintenance represents a shift from ownership to stewardship. Investors are no longer simply reacting to property failures—they are actively preserving asset value over time. Every property becomes a living system that is continuously monitored, optimized, and protected through intelligence rather than manual oversight. This transforms real estate investing from a reactive business into a proactive wealth preservation strategy.

When combined with centralized intelligence from Chapter 2, predictive maintenance becomes even more powerful. It no longer operates in isolation—it becomes part of a fully integrated portfolio system where financial data, tenant behavior, and maintenance risk all interact in real time. This creates a self-reinforcing loop of efficiency, where each improvement strengthens the entire portfolio structure.

This is the foundation of true scalability in real estate: not just acquiring assets, but preserving and optimizing them intelligently over time.

*The Property That Taught Him To See The Future*

Ethan considered himself a disciplined investor. He did everything by the book. He inspected properties, ran his numbers carefully, and always kept reserves for unexpected repairs. For years, his approach worked. His portfolio grew steadily, and his properties performed consistently. But as he expanded beyond a handful of units, something began to change.

The first sign was small. A water heater failed unexpectedly in one of his rental properties. Nothing unusual. Just a standard repair. A few weeks later, another property had a similar issue. Then another. At first, Ethan dismissed it as coincidence. Old properties simply required maintenance. That was part of the business.

But the pattern kept repeating.

Within a few months, multiple properties began experiencing similar issues—plumbing leaks, HVAC inefficiencies, appliance breakdowns. Each event on its own was manageable. But together, they created instability in his cash flow. Worse, tenants began expressing frustration. Some delayed renewing leases. Others began asking about moving out. Ethan realized he was no longer just dealing with maintenance problems. He was dealing with a system he could not see clearly.

Frustrated, he began searching for a better way to manage his portfolio. That was when he was introduced to predictive maintenance systems powered by artificial intelligence. At first, he was skeptical. The idea that software could predict when a water heater or HVAC system might fail seemed unrealistic. But he was running out of better options.

He decided to test it.

He integrated his properties into platforms like Buildium and AppFolio, allowing the system to begin collecting and analyzing maintenance data. For the first time, everything was being tracked in one place—not just expenses, but patterns, timing, frequency, and severity of issues.

At first, nothing seemed different.

Then the system began sending alerts.

One property showed a high probability of HVAC failure within the next 60 days. Another showed increasing plumbing stress based on recurring minor repair patterns. A third property, which had seemed stable, was flagged for electrical inefficiencies that had gone unnoticed for years. Ethan was surprised. These were not obvious problems. They were hidden patterns.

He followed the system's recommendations and began addressing issues proactively. Instead of waiting for failures, he replaced components early, scheduled preventative maintenance, and adjusted vendor schedules based on risk levels.

Something unexpected happened almost immediately.

Emergency repair costs dropped.

Tenant complaints decreased.

Cash flow stabilized.

But the biggest change was not financial—it was psychological.

For the first time, Ethan was not surprised by problems. He was expecting them before they happened.

As months passed, his confidence in the system grew. He stopped reacting to breakdowns entirely. Instead, he operated from a schedule of predicted maintenance events. Repairs were no longer emergencies—they were planned operations.

One evening, while reviewing his dashboard, Ethan noticed something profound. The system had accurately predicted nearly every major maintenance event in his portfolio over the past six months. Not only that, but it had also helped him avoid several costly emergency repairs entirely.

He leaned back and realized something he had never considered before:

He was no longer managing properties.

He was maintaining a system that managed them for him.

From that moment forward, Ethan stopped asking, "What broke today?"

And started asking, "What is about to break next—and how do I stop it before it happens?"

That was the moment he stopped reacting to his portfolio...

And started predicting it.

*Chapter 4*

# Ai-Powered Financial Optimization And Portfolio Performance Engineering

As a real estate portfolio expands, financial complexity increases exponentially. What once was a simple calculation of rent minus mortgage and expenses becomes a multi-layered financial ecosystem involving debt structures, tax implications, refinancing opportunities, equity positioning, insurance fluctuations, vacancy modeling, and capital allocation strategy. Most investors attempt to manage this complexity manually using spreadsheets or accounting software, but this approach quickly breaks down at scale. Chapter 4 introduces a more advanced paradigm: AI-powered financial optimization, where portfolio performance is continuously analyzed, adjusted, and engineered in real time to maximize returns and minimize inefficiencies.

At the core of financial optimization is the idea that real estate portfolios are not static—they are dynamic systems that can be actively improved through intelligent decision-making. Traditional investors tend to evaluate performance periodically, often monthly or quarterly, which creates a lag between financial reality and financial understanding. AI eliminates this delay by continuously tracking every financial movement across the portfolio. Rent collection, debt payments, maintenance costs, insurance adjustments, tax obligations, and capital expenditures are all processed in real time, creating a live financial model of the entire portfolio.

This transformation allows investors to move from reactive accounting to proactive financial engineering. Instead of asking what happened last month, investors begin to ask what should happen next. AI systems identify inefficiencies as they emerge and recommend adjustments before they negatively impact performance. For example, if a property's cash flow begins declining due to rising expenses or stagnant rent, the system can immediately flag the issue and suggest corrective actions such as rent optimization, expense restructuring, or refinancing analysis.

Platforms such as Buildium and AppFolio play a foundational role in centralizing financial data. These systems track income and expenses across properties, but when enhanced with artificial intelligence, they evolve into financial intelligence engines. Instead of simply reporting numbers, they begin interpreting them. They identify trends, compare performance across assets, and highlight opportunities for optimization that would otherwise remain hidden in raw data. One of the most powerful capabilities of AI-driven financial optimization is cash flow forecasting. In traditional real estate investing, cash flow is calculated based on static assumptions–fixed rent, estimated expenses, and projected vacancy rates. AI replaces this static model with dynamic forecasting that adjusts in real time based on actual performance data. If maintenance costs increase or rental income fluctuates, the forecast automatically updates. This provides investors with a continuously accurate financial outlook rather than a fixed snapshot that becomes outdated immediately after creation.

Another key component is debt optimization. Real estate portfolios often involve multiple layers of financing, including primary mortgages, refinancing structures, lines of credit, and sometimes private lending arrangements. Managing these debts manually becomes increasingly complex as portfolios scale. AI simplifies this by analyzing interest rates, amortization schedules, equity positions, and market conditions to identify opportunities for refinancing or restructuring. It can determine when shifting debt from one property to another improves overall portfolio cash flow or when consolidating loans reduces risk exposure.

Tax efficiency is another critical area where AI introduces significant advantages. Real estate investors often miss opportunities for tax optimization simply because the data required to identify them is fragmented or difficult to analyze manually. AI systems can categorize expenses, track depreciation schedules, and simulate tax scenarios based on different portfolio structures. This allows investors to make decisions that improve after-tax returns rather than focusing solely on gross income.

Capital allocation is also fundamentally transformed. In traditional investing, capital is often allocated based on intuition or historical performance. AI introduces a more precise approach by evaluating return on equity across all assets simultaneously. It identifies which properties are generating the highest returns relative to their equity position and which are underperforming. This allows investors to strategically redeploy capital by refinancing high-equity properties or selling underperforming assets and reinvesting into higher-yield opportunities.

Another major benefit of AI financial optimization is anomaly detection. In large portfolios, financial errors and inefficiencies often go unnoticed because they are small relative to total revenue. However, over time, these small inefficiencies can accumulate into significant losses. AI continuously scans financial data for anomalies such as unexpected expense spikes, irregular payment patterns, or inconsistent income reporting. By identifying these issues early, investors can correct them before they compound. AI also enables scenario modeling at a level that was previously impossible without dedicated financial teams. Investors can simulate different portfolio strategies and immediately see the impact on long-term performance. For example, what happens if interest rates rise by 2%? What happens if rent increases are implemented across certain markets? What happens if a portion of the portfolio is sold and reinvested into higher-growth regions? These simulations allow investors to make informed strategic decisions rather than relying on assumptions.

As portfolios scale, the importance of financial optimization increases dramatically. Small inefficiencies in a five-property portfolio may be negligible. But in a fifty-property portfolio, those same inefficiencies can translate into tens of thousands of dollars in lost income or unnecessary expenses. AI ensures that no inefficiency remains invisible, no matter how small or distributed across the portfolio it may be.

Ultimately, AI-powered financial optimization transforms real estate investing from income tracking into performance engineering. Investors are no longer simply measuring results—they are actively shaping them. Every decision becomes part of a continuous optimization cycle designed to improve cash flow, reduce risk, and increase long-term portfolio value.

This is the shift from being a property owner to becoming a financial architect. A shift from passive income to engineered income. And a shift from reacting to financial outcomes to actively designing them.

*The Investor Who Stopped Guessing And Started Optimizing Everything*

When Marcus first started investing in real estate, he believed success was simple math. Buy properties, collect rent, pay expenses, and keep the difference. For a while, that approach worked. His early portfolio of a few properties generated steady income, and he felt confident in his system. But as he expanded, something began to change.

His income stopped feeling predictable.

Some months were strong. Others were unexpectedly weak. Expenses fluctuated in ways he couldn't fully explain. Refinancing opportunities came and went without clear timing. And despite owning more properties than ever before, he felt less in control of his financial outcomes.

At first, he blamed the market. Interest rates were changing. Maintenance costs were rising. Insurance premiums were unpredictable. But deep down, he suspected something else: he wasn't actually managing his portfolio—he was just observing it after the fact. One evening, while reviewing his financial reports, Marcus realized something unsettling. He could tell exactly how much money he had made last month, but he had no idea how much more he could have made if he had optimized his decisions differently.

That realization changed everything.

Shortly after, Marcus was introduced to AI-powered financial optimization systems integrated into platforms like Buildium and AppFolio. At first, he thought they were just upgraded accounting tools. But as he began using them, he realized they were something far more powerful.

They didn't just show him what had happened.

They showed him what could have happened—and what should happen next.

The first insight shocked him.

One of his properties had significantly higher expenses than similar properties in his portfolio. Not because of a single major issue, but because of a series of small inefficiencies—overpriced vendor contracts, delayed maintenance scheduling, and minor recurring repairs that had never been addressed strategically.

Another property was underperforming in cash flow simply because rent had not been adjusted in over a year, despite strong market growth in the area.

A third property had excess equity that could be refinanced to unlock capital for higher-yield investments.

Individually, none of these issues seemed critical. But together, they represented a massive gap in performance.

Marcus acted immediately.

He renegotiated vendor contracts.

He adjusted rent prices based on AI market analysis.

He refinanced two properties and reallocated capital into a higher-performing asset.

Within months, his portfolio performance began to change dramatically.

Cash flow increased.

Expenses stabilized.

Capital efficiency improved.

But the most surprising change was not financial—it was mental.

For the first time, Marcus was not reacting to his portfolio. He was actively shaping it. Every week, the system presented him with optimization opportunities. Some were small—minor expense adjustments. Others were large—refinancing strategies or asset repositioning suggestions. But each one gave him something he had never had before: clarity.

One night, Marcus sat reviewing his dashboard and noticed something profound.

His portfolio was no longer random.

It was becoming optimized.

Continuously.

Automatically.

Intelligently.

And he realized something that changed how he viewed real estate forever:

He wasn't just earning income from properties.

He was engineering financial performance.

And the more he optimized, the more the system revealed there was still to improve.

*Chapter 5*

# Ai-Driven Tenant Intelligence And Portfolio Stability Systems

As real estate portfolios grow, one of the most influential factors determining long-term success is not property selection, financing structure, or even maintenance efficiency—it is tenant quality and tenant behavior. Every property's performance ultimately depends on the people occupying it. Tenants determine cash flow consistency, maintenance frequency, property condition, lease renewal rates, and even long-term asset appreciation. Yet in traditional real estate investing, tenant management is often treated as a reactive process rather than a strategic system. Chapter 5 introduces a new paradigm: AI-driven tenant intelligence, where tenant behavior is analyzed, predicted, and optimized to create portfolio-wide stability and predictable income.

At the foundation of tenant intelligence is data. Every interaction between a tenant and a property generates valuable information—payment timing, communication frequency, maintenance requests, lease compliance behavior, and renewal tendencies. Traditionally, this data is stored but rarely analyzed in depth. Investors may know whether a tenant pays on time, but they rarely understand the deeper behavioral patterns that predict long-term tenancy stability. AI changes this by transforming tenant data into behavioral intelligence. Instead of viewing tenants as isolated units, AI evaluates them as part of a broader behavioral ecosystem across the entire portfolio.

Platforms such as Buildium and AppFolio serve as the operational foundation for capturing tenant-level data at scale. These systems track rent payments, lease terms, maintenance requests, and communication history. When enhanced with artificial intelligence, this data becomes far more powerful. AI begins to identify patterns such as which tenants are more likely to renew leases, which tenant profiles tend to generate higher maintenance costs, and which properties attract the most stable long-term occupants.

One of the most powerful applications of AI tenant intelligence is risk prediction. In traditional property management, tenant risk is often identified only after problems arise—late payments, lease violations, or property damage. AI enables early detection of risk signals long before they escalate. For example, subtle changes in payment timing, increased maintenance requests, or shifts in communication behavior can all indicate potential future instability. By identifying these patterns early, investors can proactively intervene, adjust lease strategies, or prepare for turnover before financial disruption occurs. This predictive capability fundamentally changes portfolio stability. Instead of experiencing unpredictable tenant turnover, investors begin to see tenant behavior as something measurable and manageable. AI systems can assign behavioral risk scores to tenants based on historical data and real-time activity. These scores help investors prioritize attention, improve tenant screening processes, and reduce overall portfolio volatility. Over time, this leads to more consistent occupancy rates and more predictable income streams.

Another major transformation comes in tenant screening and acquisition. Traditionally, tenant selection relies heavily on credit scores, income verification, and rental history. While these metrics are useful, they do not always capture long-term behavioral reliability. AI expands this process by analyzing broader data sets, including payment patterns across multiple properties, historical lease behavior, and even macro-level demographic trends. This allows investors to identify tenants who are not just qualified, but statistically more likely to remain stable over time.

AI also improves lease structure optimization. Different tenant types respond differently to lease terms. Some tenants prefer longer leases with stable rent, while others may respond better to flexible terms or incremental rent adjustments. By analyzing historical tenant behavior across the portfolio, AI can recommend optimal lease structures for different property types and tenant profiles. This increases renewal rates and reduces vacancy periods between leases.

Maintenance behavior is another critical component of tenant intelligence. Some tenants generate higher maintenance costs not because of property issues, but because of usage patterns. AI can detect correlations between tenant behavior and maintenance frequency, helping investors distinguish between property-related issues and tenant-related usage patterns. This insight allows for more accurate budgeting, better tenant placement strategies, and improved property longevity.

Communication intelligence is also a key element of AI-driven tenant systems. Tenant communication is often inconsistent and time-consuming for property owners. AI systems can analyze communication patterns to identify urgency, sentiment, and potential escalation risk. For example, repeated maintenance inquiries or emotionally charged messages may indicate dissatisfaction that could lead to lease termination. By detecting these signals early, investors can intervene proactively and improve tenant retention.

One of the most valuable outcomes of tenant intelligence is portfolio stabilization. In real estate investing, volatility is one of the biggest threats to long-term success. Vacancies, late payments, unexpected turnover, and maintenance spikes all contribute to financial instability. AI reduces this volatility by creating a more predictable tenant ecosystem. When tenant behavior is understood and managed proactively, the entire portfolio becomes more stable and resilient.

Tenant intelligence also plays a direct role in scaling. As portfolios grow, managing tenant relationships manually becomes impossible. AI ensures that tenant management scales seamlessly alongside portfolio growth. Whether an investor has ten tenants or one hundred, the system continuously monitors behavior, flags risks, and provides actionable insights without increasing workload. This allows investors to scale without losing control over tenant quality or portfolio stability.

Ultimately, AI-driven tenant intelligence transforms property management from reactive administration into predictive relationship management. Investors are no longer simply responding to tenant behavior—they are understanding it, anticipating it, and optimizing it across the entire portfolio. This shift creates a more stable, more predictable, and more profitable real estate business.

Tenant intelligence is not just about reducing problems—it is about creating alignment between property performance and human behavior. When tenants are well-matched, well-managed, and well-understood, the entire portfolio performs better. Income stabilizes. Expenses decrease. Turnover declines. And long-term value increases.

This is the foundation of scalable real estate investing: not just owning properties, but understanding the people who make those properties perform.

*The Tenant Patterns He Couldn't See Until The System Showed Him*

Ethan thought he was a good property manager. He responded to tenant requests quickly, kept units well maintained, and made sure rent was collected on time. His portfolio of rental properties had grown steadily over the years, and on the surface, everything seemed stable. But as his portfolio expanded, subtle problems began to appear.

Some properties had higher turnover than others. Certain tenants seemed to move out just as leases ended. Maintenance costs varied unpredictably between similar units. And occasionally, he would experience clusters of late payments that didn't seem connected to any obvious external factor.

At first, Ethan assumed it was normal variation. Real estate always had some unpredictability. But over time, the inconsistencies became harder to ignore. One property might perform flawlessly for months, while another similar property experienced repeated tenant issues. The patterns didn't make sense.

Frustrated, Ethan decided to dig deeper. That was when he discovered AI-driven tenant intelligence systems built into platforms like Buildium and AppFolio.

At first, he used them just to organize tenant data. But slowly, something unexpected happened—the system started revealing patterns he had never noticed before.

One tenant group consistently paid rent earlier and stayed longer than others. Another group had slightly higher maintenance requests but also higher renewal rates. A third group showed subtle signs of late payment behavior months before actually becoming delinquent.

These patterns had always existed—but Ethan had never been able to see them.

The system went further.

It began assigning behavioral risk indicators to tenants based on historical and real-time data. One tenant in a seemingly stable property was flagged for increasing risk based on communication delays and inconsistent payment timing.

Another tenant, previously considered average, was identified as highly stable due to consistent long-term behavior patterns across multiple metrics.

Ethan was stunned.

For the first time, tenant management was not guesswork. It was analysis.

He started acting on the insights.

He adjusted screening criteria for new tenants.

He proactively engaged tenants flagged for potential turnover risk.

He restructured lease terms in properties with higher instability patterns.

The results were immediate.

Turnover decreased.

Late payments dropped.

Maintenance complaints became more predictable and manageable.

But the most surprising change was not operational—it was emotional. For years, Ethan had felt like he was constantly reacting to tenant problems. Now, he felt like he was anticipating them before they happened. One evening, he reviewed his portfolio dashboard and noticed something profound.

His properties were no longer behaving randomly.

They were forming patterns.

Predictable patterns.

Understandable patterns.

Manageable patterns.

And for the first time, Ethan realized something important:

His tenants were not the source of unpredictability.

His lack of visibility was.

Now that he could see clearly, everything changed.

He wasn't chasing tenant problems anymore.

He was preventing them before they ever began.

*Chapter 6*

# Ai-Driven Scaling Systems And Multi-Market Portfolio Expansion

Once a real estate investor reaches a certain level of portfolio maturity, the challenge is no longer how to manage properties effectively, but how to scale without breaking the system that made those properties successful in the first place. Scaling is where many investors fail—not because they lack capital or opportunity, but because their operational systems cannot handle increased complexity. Chapter 6 introduces the concept of AI-driven scaling systems, where growth is no longer constrained by human capacity, but instead guided and stabilized by intelligent automation that allows portfolios to expand across multiple markets without losing control, visibility, or efficiency.

At its core, scaling in real estate is a systems problem, not a capital problem. Most investors believe that more money equals more properties, and more properties equals more wealth. While this is partially true, it ignores the operational strain that comes with growth. Each new property introduces additional tenants, maintenance requirements, financial data, legal obligations, and market variables. Without a scalable system, each layer of growth adds exponential complexity. AI changes this dynamic by standardizing and automating the operational backbone of the portfolio, ensuring that each new asset integrates seamlessly into an existing intelligent framework rather than creating additional friction.

Central to this scalable framework are property management systems such as Buildium and AppFolio. These platforms provide the structural foundation for managing large portfolios, but when enhanced with artificial intelligence, they become far more than administrative tools. They evolve into adaptive systems capable of handling increased volume without increasing workload. Every new property added to the portfolio is automatically absorbed into the system, where data flows, tenant communication, financial tracking, and maintenance workflows are instantly aligned with existing operational structures.

AI-driven scaling begins with standardization. Before a portfolio can grow efficiently, its systems must become uniform. Lease structures, tenant screening criteria, maintenance workflows, financial reporting formats, and communication protocols must all be consistent. AI helps enforce this consistency by identifying deviations and automatically correcting them or flagging them for adjustment. This ensures that as the portfolio expands, it does not become fragmented or inconsistent across different properties or markets.

Once standardization is established, AI introduces automation at scale. Instead of manually managing each property, investors operate through centralized systems that execute repetitive tasks automatically. Rent collection, lease reminders, maintenance scheduling, and financial reporting are handled without manual intervention. This allows investors to focus on strategic decisions rather than operational execution. As more properties are added, automation simply extends to include them without requiring additional effort.

A key component of AI-driven scaling is market expansion intelligence. Traditional investors expand into new markets based on intuition, local knowledge, or anecdotal data. AI introduces a data-driven approach to expansion by analyzing macroeconomic trends, rental demand, population growth, employment data, and property appreciation patterns across multiple regions. This allows investors to identify emerging markets before they become saturated, enabling early entry into high-growth areas with reduced competition and higher potential returns.

In addition to identifying markets, AI also evaluates scalability risk. Not all markets are suitable for rapid portfolio expansion.

Some may have regulatory constraints, volatile rental demand, or high maintenance costs. AI analyzes these factors in real time, providing investors with a risk-adjusted view of expansion opportunities. This ensures that scaling decisions are not just based on potential returns, but also on long-term stability and operational feasibility.

Another major advantage of AI-driven scaling is portfolio balancing. As portfolios grow across multiple markets, performance variability increases. Some markets may outperform while others underperform due to local economic conditions. AI continuously evaluates portfolio balance and recommends adjustments to optimize overall performance. This may include reallocating capital, adjusting acquisition strategies, or divesting from underperforming regions. The goal is not just growth, but optimized growth across the entire portfolio.

Financial scalability is also significantly enhanced through AI systems. As portfolios expand, financial complexity increases due to varying property values, loan structures, tax obligations, and cash flow dynamics. AI simplifies this by aggregating all financial data into a unified model that updates in real time. Investors can see not only individual property performance but also consolidated portfolio performance across all markets. This allows for faster, more informed decision-making at scale. Another critical element is operational delegation. In traditional real estate investing, scaling often requires hiring more staff, property managers, and contractors. This increases overhead and introduces human variability into the system. AI reduces dependency on human management by automating decision-making processes and standardizing operations. While human oversight is still necessary, the reliance on manual coordination decreases significantly as AI handles more of the operational workload.

AI also enhances scalability through predictive workload management. As portfolios grow, operational demand increases, but not in a linear fashion. Some properties require more attention than others depending on tenant behavior, maintenance cycles, and market conditions. AI predicts workload distribution across the portfolio and helps investors allocate resources efficiently. This prevents bottlenecks and ensures that scaling does not overwhelm the operational system.

Perhaps one of the most transformative aspects of AI-driven scaling is the ability to operate across multiple markets simultaneously with minimal additional complexity. In traditional models, expanding into new geographic regions introduces new laws, market dynamics, service providers, and management challenges. AI reduces this friction by standardizing operational processes and adapting them dynamically to local conditions. This allows investors to manage geographically diverse portfolios as if they were operating within a single unified system.

Ultimately, AI-driven scaling represents the transition from manual portfolio growth to intelligent expansion architecture. Investors are no longer constrained by their ability to personally oversee each property or market. Instead, they build systems that scale independently of their attention. Growth becomes a function of system design rather than personal capacity.

This is the true breakthrough in modern real estate investing: the ability to expand without increasing complexity, to grow without losing control, and to scale without breaking the system.

### *The Investor Who Learned How To Grow Without Getting Busier*

When Lucas first started investing in real estate, he believed scaling meant working harder. More properties meant more tenants, more maintenance, more decisions, and more responsibility. For years, that belief held true. His first few properties were manageable, but as he expanded, his workload grew rapidly. Every new acquisition added complexity, and soon, he found himself constantly reacting to issues instead of planning growth. At fifteen properties, Lucas felt in control but busy. At twenty-five, he felt overwhelmed. At thirty, he realized something uncomfortable: he was no longer scaling his business—his business was scaling his stress.

Every new market he entered introduced new challenges. Different property laws, different contractors, different tenant expectations. What worked in one city did not always work in another. His systems, once reliable, began to strain under the weight of expansion.

One evening, after spending hours trying to coordinate issues across three different markets, Lucas sat back and asked himself a difficult question: if growth keeps making my life harder, am I actually building wealth or just building complexity?

That question changed everything.

Shortly after, Lucas was introduced to AI-driven scaling systems integrated into platforms like Buildium and AppFolio. At first, he thought they were just better property management tools. But as he began exploring them, he realized they represented something much bigger: a way to scale without increasing operational chaos.

He started small.

He standardized his lease structures.

He unified his maintenance workflows.

He centralized his financial reporting.

At first, nothing seemed dramatically different. But over time, something remarkable happened—his portfolio stopped feeling like separate properties and started feeling like one interconnected system.

Then he expanded again.

This time, something changed.

Instead of feeling overwhelmed by new properties, Lucas noticed that each new acquisition simply plugged into his existing system. Tenant communication was automated. Maintenance workflows were standardized. Financial reporting updated automatically. There was no breakdown in structure, no increase in confusion, and no rise in stress.

For the first time, growth did not feel heavier.

It felt lighter.

Encouraged, Lucas expanded into a new market. Then another. Then another.

Each time, the system absorbed the new properties without disruption.

One day, Lucas realized something unusual: he was managing more properties than ever before, yet working fewer hours than he had years earlier.

Curious, he reviewed his dashboard. It showed properties across multiple states, each performing within expected ranges. Maintenance was being handled proactively. Tenants were stable. Financial performance was consistent across markets.

Everything was working without constant intervention.

That was when it clicked.

He was no longer scaling manually.

He was scaling through systems.

And the system was doing the heavy lifting.

One evening, Lucas sat quietly and reflected on how much had changed. He remembered the early days when every new property meant more stress, more calls, and more problems.

Now, new properties meant almost nothing in terms of operational burden.

The system handled it.

He no longer asked, “How many properties can I manage?” Instead, he asked, “How far can the system scale?”

And for the first time in his investing career, he realized something powerful:

He was no longer growing his workload.

He was growing his system.

And that system could grow far beyond him.

## Chapter 7

# Ai Short-Term Rental Intelligence And Dynamic Revenue Optimization

Short-term rental investing represents one of the most dynamic and data-sensitive sectors in real estate. Unlike long-term rentals, where income is relatively stable and predictable, short-term rentals operate in a constantly shifting environment influenced by seasonality, local demand, tourism trends, pricing competition, reviews, and platform algorithms. Because of this variability, traditional management approaches often fall short at scale. Chapter 7 introduces AI-powered short-term rental intelligence, a system designed to optimize pricing, occupancy, guest experience, and revenue performance in real time across a growing portfolio of Airbnb-style properties.

At the core of short-term rental success is one critical variable: revenue per available night. Unlike traditional rentals that rely on fixed monthly income, short-term rentals require continuous optimization to ensure each night is priced correctly based on demand. Without optimization, properties either underprice and lose revenue or overprice and lose occupancy. AI solves this problem by continuously analyzing market data, competitor listings, seasonal trends, and local demand signals to dynamically adjust pricing strategies. This transforms pricing from a static decision into a living system that evolves daily.

Platforms like Airbnb and data intelligence tools such as AirDNA form the foundation of short-term rental analytics. These systems collect massive amounts of data on occupancy rates, pricing trends, and market performance across thousands of listings. When enhanced with AI, this data becomes predictive rather than descriptive. Instead of simply showing what competitors are charging, AI forecasts what they will charge, what demand will look like in the coming weeks, and how pricing should adjust to maximize both occupancy and revenue.

One of the most powerful applications of AI in short-term rentals is dynamic pricing optimization. Traditional hosts often rely on fixed pricing strategies or manual adjustments based on intuition. This approach fails to capture real-time market fluctuations. AI continuously adjusts pricing based on multiple variables including local events, weather patterns, booking lead times, day-of-week trends, and competitor occupancy levels. This ensures that every available night is priced at its optimal revenue point, maximizing total income without sacrificing occupancy rates. Another key component of AI-driven short-term rental management is occupancy forecasting. Predicting occupancy is significantly more complex than predicting long-term rental stability because demand fluctuates daily. AI models analyze historical booking patterns, seasonal cycles, and external demand indicators such as tourism traffic, flight trends, and local events to forecast future occupancy levels with high accuracy. This allows investors to proactively adjust marketing strategies, pricing structures, and minimum stay requirements to maintain optimal booking flow.

Guest experience optimization is another critical factor that directly impacts short-term rental performance. Unlike long-term tenants, short-term guests rely heavily on reviews, communication quality, and overall experience. AI enhances guest experience management by automating communication, personalizing messaging, and predicting potential guest issues before they occur. For example, if a guest is likely to arrive late or request additional amenities based on behavior patterns, AI can proactively trigger personalized responses or operational adjustments to improve satisfaction.

AI also plays a major role in review optimization. In short-term rentals, reviews directly impact ranking visibility and future bookings. Poor reviews can significantly reduce occupancy rates, while strong reviews increase platform ranking and demand. AI analyzes guest feedback patterns to identify recurring issues, highlight strengths, and recommend operational improvements that lead to higher satisfaction scores. Over time, this creates a feedback loop where each improvement increases visibility, which increases bookings, which increases revenue.

Another important aspect of AI-driven short-term rental intelligence is portfolio diversification across markets. Unlike traditional rentals, short-term rental performance varies significantly by location. Some markets are highly seasonal, while others maintain consistent demand year-round. AI evaluates market performance across multiple regions and recommends optimal expansion strategies based on demand stability, regulatory conditions, and revenue potential. This allows investors to build diversified portfolios that reduce risk while maximizing income consistency.

Operational automation is also essential in scaling short-term rental portfolios. Managing multiple properties manually becomes nearly impossible due to constant guest turnover, cleaning schedules, check-in coordination, and maintenance requirements. AI automates these processes by coordinating cleaning teams, scheduling turnovers, managing guest communications, and tracking operational workflows. This reduces dependency on manual coordination and ensures consistent guest experience across all properties. Financial performance tracking in short-term rentals is also significantly enhanced through AI systems. Instead of reviewing monthly reports, investors receive real-time insights into revenue performance, occupancy efficiency, and profit margins per property. AI can identify which properties are underperforming due to pricing inefficiencies, operational issues, or demand fluctuations. It can also recommend specific actions to improve performance, such as adjusting minimum stay requirements or repositioning listings within the market.

One of the most powerful advantages of AI in short-term rentals is the ability to scale without losing quality control. As portfolios grow, maintaining consistent guest experience becomes increasingly difficult. AI ensures that every property follows standardized operational protocols while still adapting dynamically to local market conditions. This balance between standardization and flexibility allows investors to scale aggressively without sacrificing performance or reputation.

Ultimately, AI short-term rental intelligence transforms vacation rental investing from reactive management into real-time revenue engineering. Every listing becomes part of a dynamic system that continuously optimizes itself for occupancy, pricing, and guest satisfaction. Investors are no longer managing individual properties—they are managing a network of high-performance revenue engines. This is the evolution of short-term rental investing: from manual hosting to automated revenue optimization systems that operate continuously across multiple markets.

*The Night His Airbnb Business Stopped Being Manual*

When Adrian first started investing in short-term rentals, he thought it was the easiest path to cash flow. The numbers looked simple: buy a property, list it on Airbnb, and watch the income come in. And for a while, it worked exactly like that. His first property performed well. Then his second. Then his third.

But everything changed when he reached ten properties.

Suddenly, nothing felt simple anymore.

He was managing pricing for multiple listings, responding to guest messages at all hours, coordinating cleaners across different schedules, and trying to adjust rates based on intuition and experience. Some properties were fully booked while others sat empty. Some months were highly profitable, while others felt unpredictable and inconsistent.

The biggest problem wasn't income–it was control.

Adrian realized he was constantly reacting to his business instead of directing it.

One evening, after missing a surge pricing opportunity during a local event, he sat down frustrated. He had left thousands of dollars on the table simply because he did not adjust pricing in time. That was the moment he realized something had to change.

Shortly after, Adrian discovered AI-driven short-term rental systems powered by platforms like Airbnb and analytics tools like AirDNA.

At first, he was skeptical. He had always trusted his instincts and experience. But curiosity pushed him forward.

He integrated his listings into an AI-powered system.

The first thing it changed was pricing.

Instead of manually adjusting nightly rates, the system began optimizing prices automatically. When demand increased in his city due to a weekend festival, prices adjusted upward instantly. When demand dropped midweek, prices adjusted downward to maintain occupancy. He no longer had to guess. The system was doing it for him.

Then something even more surprising happened.

Occupancy rates improved.

Revenue increased.

But Adrian hadn't changed anything manually. The system was learning, adapting, and optimizing in real time.

Next came guest communication.

Messages that once took hours to manage were now automated, personalized, and timed perfectly. Guests received clear check-in instructions, follow-ups, and support responses without delay. Complaints decreased. Reviews improved.

Adrian began to feel something unfamiliar.

Relief.

For the first time, his business wasn't controlling him.

It was supporting him.

As months passed, Adrian expanded again. More properties were added. In the past, this would have meant more stress, more complexity, and more late nights managing operations.

But this time was different.

Each new property was absorbed into the system instantly.

Pricing adjusted automatically.

Occupancy was optimized.

Operations were coordinated without manual effort.

One night, Adrian checked his dashboard and noticed something striking.

He was earning more income than ever before, but spending less time managing his business than when he had just a few properties.

He leaned back and realized something profound.

He was no longer running short-term rentals.

He was running a system that ran them for him.

And the more he expanded, the more efficient it became.

That was the moment Adrian understood the truth:

Short-term rental success wasn't about working harder.

It was about building a system that never stopped optimizing.

*Chapter 8*

# Ai-Powered Real Estate Financing Intelligence And Capital Optimization Systems

In real estate investing, financing is often treated as a one-time event rather than a continuous strategic advantage. Most investors focus heavily on acquisition, deal analysis, or property management, but overlook the fact that financing structure is one of the most powerful determinants of long-term wealth creation. The difference between average returns and exceptional portfolio growth is often not the properties themselves, but how those properties are financed, refinanced, and optimized over time. Chapter 8 introduces AI-powered financing intelligence, a system that continuously analyzes lending options, capital structures, and refinancing opportunities to maximize leverage efficiency and long-term portfolio performance.

Traditional real estate financing is fragmented. Investors typically secure loans based on immediate needs, compare limited lender options manually, and make decisions based on static information. Once a loan is closed, it is often left untouched for years, even if market conditions change significantly. This creates inefficiencies where investors may be locked into suboptimal rates, underutilized equity, or outdated financing structures. AI transforms this by turning financing into a dynamic, ongoing optimization process rather than a one-time transaction.

At the core of financing intelligence is real-time market analysis. AI continuously monitors interest rates, lending guidelines, loan program changes, and capital market conditions to identify opportunities for improvement. Instead of relying on periodic refinancing reviews, the system constantly evaluates whether a better financing structure is available. If interest rates drop, if equity increases significantly, or if new loan programs become available, AI immediately flags these opportunities and calculates their impact on the investor's portfolio.

Platforms such as Buildium and broader financial tools integrated with lending systems help centralize property and financial data, but AI adds the intelligence layer that connects financing decisions directly to portfolio performance. It does not just show loan balances—it evaluates how each loan affects cash flow, return on equity, and long-term scalability. This allows investors to treat financing as a strategic lever rather than a passive obligation. One of the most powerful applications of AI financing intelligence is refinancing optimization. In traditional investing, refinancing decisions are often delayed due to complexity, uncertainty, or lack of awareness. AI eliminates this friction by continuously analyzing loan performance against current market conditions. If refinancing a property reduces monthly payments, increases cash flow, or unlocks usable equity, the system immediately presents this opportunity with detailed projections. This ensures that capital is never left idle or inefficiently structured for long periods.

Another key component is leverage optimization. Real estate wealth is heavily influenced by how effectively investors use debt to control assets. However, improper leverage can increase risk, while underutilized leverage can limit growth. AI balances this equation by analyzing debt-to-income ratios, loan-to-value structures, and portfolio-wide leverage exposure. It identifies when additional leverage can safely accelerate growth and when reducing debt exposure may improve stability. This creates a more intelligent approach to scaling that adapts to both market conditions and investor goals.

AI also plays a major role in lender comparison and loan selection. Traditionally, investors rely on brokers or manual research to compare loan products, which often leads to incomplete analysis or missed opportunities. AI aggregates lending options across multiple sources, evaluates terms in real time, and ranks financing options based on long-term portfolio impact rather than just short-term interest rates. This ensures that every financing decision is optimized for overall wealth creation rather than isolated cost savings.

Another transformative capability is equity intelligence. As properties appreciate or debt is paid down, equity accumulates across the portfolio. However, many investors fail to actively leverage this growing equity. AI continuously tracks equity positions across all properties and identifies opportunities to redeploy capital. This may include cash-out refinancing, HELOC utilization, or strategic restructuring of assets to unlock liquidity for further investments. Instead of letting equity sit idle, AI transforms it into an active growth engine.

Risk management is also deeply integrated into financing intelligence. Overleveraging, interest rate exposure, and market volatility can all impact portfolio stability. AI continuously monitors these risks and provides early warning signals when financing structures become imbalanced. For example, if a portfolio becomes too heavily dependent on variable-rate loans during rising interest rate environments, the system can recommend restructuring strategies to reduce exposure. This ensures that growth does not come at the expense of financial stability. AI financing systems also enable scenario simulation at a portfolio level. Investors can model different financing strategies and immediately see their impact on cash flow, equity growth, and long-term returns. For example, what happens if multiple properties are refinanced simultaneously? What if equity is extracted and reinvested into higher-yield assets? What if debt is reduced across certain segments of the portfolio? These simulations allow investors to make informed capital decisions with full visibility into future outcomes.

As portfolios scale, financing becomes increasingly complex due to multiple loan types, varying interest rates, and staggered maturity schedules. AI simplifies this complexity by centralizing all financing data into a unified system. Instead of managing individual loans separately, investors gain a holistic view of portfolio-wide capital structure. This allows for more strategic decision-making that aligns financing with long-term investment goals.

Ultimately, AI-powered financing intelligence transforms real estate investing from passive borrowing into active capital engineering. Every loan becomes a strategic tool. Every refinancing opportunity becomes a potential growth accelerator. And every equity position becomes a resource for expansion. Investors are no longer simply owners of property—they become architects of capital flow. This is the evolution of real estate financing: from static debt management to dynamic capital optimization systems that continuously enhance portfolio performance.

*The Day He Stopped Thinking Like A Borrower And Started Thinking Like A Capital Engineer*

When Jason first entered real estate investing, he thought financing was just a necessary step. You found a property, got a loan, closed the deal, and moved on. That was how everyone around him operated, and for his early deals, it worked fine. He secured mortgages, collected rent, and slowly built a small portfolio that generated steady income.

But as Jason grew his portfolio, something began to feel off.

Even though his properties were performing well, his financial growth felt slower than expected. He was making money, but not optimizing it. His loans were spread across different lenders. His interest rates varied widely. Some properties had significant equity, but he wasn't actively using it. He had assets—but not leverage efficiency.

One evening, while reviewing his financials, Jason realized something uncomfortable: he didn't actually know if his financing structure was helping him grow or holding him back.

That realization changed everything.

Shortly after, Jason was introduced to AI-powered financing intelligence systems that integrated with real estate data platforms and portfolio tools like Buildium. At first, he assumed it was just another analytics dashboard. But what he discovered was something far more powerful.

The system didn't just show him his loans.

It evaluated them.

It analyzed them.

It optimized them.

For the first time, Jason could see how each loan affected his entire portfolio—not just individually, but collectively. One property had a high interest rate that was quietly draining cash flow. Another had significant equity that could be extracted and redeployed. A third property was eligible for refinancing under better market conditions he had not even considered.

The system began presenting recommendations.

Refinance this property to reduce monthly expenses.

Extract equity from this asset to fund new acquisitions.

Restructure this loan to improve portfolio cash flow.

At first, Jason was hesitant. Refinancing meant paperwork, effort, and uncertainty. But the numbers were undeniable. Each recommendation showed clear financial benefit. So he acted.

One by one, he refinanced properties.

He restructured debt.

He unlocked equity.

And something began to shift.

His cash flow improved.

His capital became more liquid.

His ability to invest increased.

But the biggest change was not financial—it was mental.

Jason stopped thinking about individual loans.

He started thinking about capital flow.

As months passed, the system continued to evolve. It tracked interest rate changes, monitored equity positions, and constantly searched for better financing structures. Jason no longer had to wonder if he was making the right decision—the system showed him what the optimal decision was.

One night, Jason looked at his updated portfolio summary and realized something powerful.

He wasn't just collecting rent anymore.

He was controlling capital.

Every property was a financial instrument.

Every loan was a strategic tool.

And every decision was part of a larger optimization system.

He leaned back and thought about how he used to see financing as something he simply "got through" when buying a property.

Now he understood something completely different:

Financing wasn't a step in investing.

It was the engine of investing.

And once he learned how to optimize that engine, his entire portfolio began to move faster than he ever thought possible.

*Chapter 9*

# Ai Portfolio Operating Systems And Fully Automated Real Estate Ecosystems

At this stage of real estate investing, the conversation is no longer about individual tools, isolated strategies, or even portfolio optimization in separate categories. Once investors reach a certain level of scale, the real challenge becomes integration. How do all the systems—acquisitions, financing, tenant management, maintenance, financial tracking, and scaling strategies—work together as one unified structure? Chapter 9 introduces the concept of AI portfolio operating systems, where every component of a real estate business is connected into a single intelligent ecosystem that runs continuously, adapts automatically, and improves over time without constant manual intervention.

An AI portfolio operating system is not just software—it is an architecture. It is the structure that connects every part of a real estate business into a synchronized, self-adjusting framework. In traditional investing, each function operates separately. Acquisition decisions are made in isolation from financing decisions. Financing is disconnected from property management. Property management is disconnected from financial forecasting. This fragmentation creates inefficiency, delays, and missed opportunities. AI eliminates this fragmentation by creating a unified system where every decision is informed by every other component in real time.

At the foundation of this system are integrated platforms such as Buildium and AppFolio, which serve as operational hubs for managing properties, tenants, and financial data. However, when enhanced with artificial intelligence, these platforms evolve far beyond administrative tools. They become living systems that process data continuously, identify patterns automatically, and make recommendations that align with portfolio-wide goals. Instead of managing individual tasks, investors begin managing an intelligent ecosystem that manages those tasks for them.

The key transformation in an AI portfolio operating system is the shift from task-based management to system-based intelligence. In traditional real estate operations, investors focus on completing tasks: finding deals, closing loans, responding to tenants, scheduling maintenance, and reviewing financial reports. Each task requires attention and decision-making. In an AI-driven system, these tasks are no longer managed individually. Instead, they are automated, prioritized, and executed within a structured workflow that adjusts dynamically based on portfolio conditions. This system operates through continuous data integration. Every event within the portfolio generates data—rent payments, maintenance requests, lease expirations, refinancing opportunities, market changes, and tenant behavior patterns. Instead of storing this data in separate systems, AI aggregates it into a unified intelligence layer. This allows the system to understand not just what is happening in one part of the portfolio, but how every part interacts with every other part.

One of the most powerful capabilities of AI portfolio operating systems is autonomous decision support. Instead of requiring investors to analyze data and make decisions manually, the system presents optimized recommendations based on real-time conditions. For example, if a property's performance declines due to rising expenses, the system may recommend rent adjustments, refinancing options, or expense restructuring. If a market shows strong appreciation trends, it may recommend acquisition opportunities before prices rise further. These recommendations are not static—they evolve continuously as new data enters the system.

Another critical function is workflow automation. In a traditional real estate business, workflows such as tenant onboarding, lease renewals, maintenance coordination, and financial reporting require manual oversight. In an AI operating system, these workflows are fully automated. Tenant applications are processed, screened, and approved through standardized criteria. Lease renewals are triggered automatically based on tenant behavior and market conditions. Maintenance requests are categorized, prioritized, and assigned without human intervention. This reduces operational load while increasing consistency and accuracy.

Financial integration is also central to the operating system. Instead of reviewing separate reports for each property, investors receive consolidated financial intelligence across the entire portfolio. Cash flow, debt structure, equity positions, and return on investment are tracked in real time. AI identifies inefficiencies, highlights opportunities, and continuously recalibrates financial forecasts based on actual performance. This transforms financial management from periodic analysis into continuous optimization.

Another defining feature of AI portfolio operating systems is adaptive scaling. As new properties are added to the portfolio, the system automatically integrates them into existing workflows. There is no need to rebuild processes or adjust management structures manually. Each new asset becomes part of the existing ecosystem instantly, inheriting standardized processes and contributing to overall intelligence. This allows portfolios to scale without increasing complexity or operational burden. Risk management is also deeply embedded into the system. AI continuously monitors portfolio exposure across multiple dimensions—financial risk, tenant risk, market risk, and operational risk. If any area begins to show instability, the system flags it immediately and recommends corrective action. This proactive approach ensures that risks are identified and addressed before they escalate into serious problems.

Over time, AI portfolio operating systems develop what can be described as institutional memory. They learn from every decision, every outcome, and every adjustment made within the portfolio. This learning process improves future recommendations and increases system accuracy. The portfolio effectively becomes smarter over time, not because of human input alone, but because of continuous machine learning across all operational layers.

Ultimately, Chapter 9 represents the transition from managing a real estate portfolio to operating a real estate intelligence system. Investors are no longer reacting to individual problems or making isolated decisions. Instead, they are overseeing a fully integrated ecosystem that handles operations, finances, tenants, and growth simultaneously. The role of the investor evolves from operator to system architect.

This is the point where real estate investing becomes truly scalable. Not because there is less work, but because the work is absorbed into an intelligent structure that executes, adapts, and improves continuously.

*The Investor Who Stopped Running His Business And Started Designing It*

When Caleb started investing in real estate, he thought success meant staying involved. He believed that the best investors were the ones who stayed closest to their properties, closest to their tenants, and closest to their numbers. So that's exactly what he did. He answered every message personally, reviewed every expense carefully, and made every decision himself.

At first, it worked.

His small portfolio was manageable, and he felt in control. But as he added more properties, things started to change. The systems he had built began to break under pressure. He found himself switching between spreadsheets, apps, emails, and phone calls just to stay updated. The more he grew, the more scattered everything became.

Eventually, Caleb realized something uncomfortable: he wasn't scaling a business. He was scaling complexity.

One evening, after spending hours trying to reconcile financial reports across multiple properties, he closed his laptop and sat in silence. He wasn't frustrated anymore—he was exhausted.

That was the moment he asked himself a question he had avoided for years: what if the way I'm doing this is the problem?

Not long after, Caleb was introduced to AI portfolio operating systems integrated through platforms like Buildium and AppFolio. At first, he didn't fully understand what made them different. He had used property management software before. It helped, but it still required constant input and oversight.

This was different.

When he began integrating his portfolio into the system, something unexpected happened.

Everything started connecting.

His tenant data, financial data, maintenance workflows, and leasing processes were no longer separate systems—they became one unified structure. Instead of jumping between tools, he saw everything in one place. More importantly, the system didn't just display information. It analyzed it.

The first change came in maintenance.

Tasks were automatically categorized, prioritized, and assigned. Tenants received faster responses. Costs became more predictable. Problems stopped escalating unnoticed.

Then came finance. The system began highlighting inefficiencies across his portfolio. One property had consistently lower returns due to hidden expense patterns. Another had strong equity but weak cash flow. A third was positioned in a market that was outperforming expectations.

Caleb didn't have to search for these insights.

They were presented to him.

Then the system began doing something even more powerful—it started making recommendations.

Refinance this property.

Adjust rent here.

Reallocate attention there.

At first, Caleb hesitated. He wasn't used to trusting a system with decisions he had always made manually. But the logic was undeniable. Every recommendation was backed by clear data and projected outcomes.

So he followed it.

Slowly, things began to change.

His workload decreased.

His clarity increased. His portfolio performance improved.

But the most surprising change wasn't financial—it was structural.

Caleb realized he wasn't managing separate properties anymore.

He was managing a system that managed them.

As time passed, the system became more intelligent. It learned from his decisions. It adapted to his preferences. It improved its recommendations based on outcomes. The more he used it, the smarter it became.

One night, Caleb opened his dashboard and paused.

Everything was running.

Tenant workflows were active.

Financial reports were updated.

Maintenance operations were moving forward.

And he hadn't touched anything in hours.

That was when it hit him.

He wasn't running his business anymore.

He was designing it.

And the system was executing it.

For the first time in his investing career, Caleb understood something deeply:

Scaling wasn't about doing more.

It was about building something that could do everything without needing him to hold it together.

And once that system was in place, his role changed forever—from operator to architect.

Chapter 10

# The Fully Autonomous Ai Real Estate Business And Wealth Machine

At the highest level of real estate investing, there is a point where the traditional definition of a portfolio no longer applies. What begins as a collection of properties eventually evolves into something far more powerful—a fully integrated, self-optimizing business system that operates continuously without requiring constant human intervention. Chapter 10 represents the final stage of this transformation: the fully autonomous AI real estate business, where acquisition, financing, operations, tenant management, maintenance, financial optimization, and scaling all function as one intelligent, self-adjusting wealth system.

This stage is not about working harder, nor is it about simply delegating tasks. It is about designing a structure where decision-making itself becomes automated, guided by data, logic, and continuous learning. In traditional real estate investing, every major decision requires human input. Investors must decide when to buy, when to sell, how to finance, how to manage, and how to scale. In an AI-driven autonomous system, these decisions are no longer isolated events. They become part of a continuous flow of intelligence that evaluates conditions in real time and executes actions based on pre-defined strategic parameters.

At the core of this system is integration across every operational layer. Platforms such as Buildium and AppFolio serve as foundational infrastructure, but the autonomous system goes far beyond property management. It connects acquisition pipelines, financing structures, tenant behavior models, maintenance prediction engines, and financial optimization algorithms into one unified intelligence layer. Instead of operating as separate departments, each function becomes part of a synchronized ecosystem that communicates continuously and adjusts dynamically.

One of the most important aspects of an autonomous real estate system is decision automation. In early stages of investing, decisions are manual and reactive. Investors analyze deals, review loans, evaluate tenants, and respond to maintenance issues individually. In an autonomous system, these decisions are governed by intelligent rules and predictive models. For example, if a property meets specific cash flow and risk criteria, the system can automatically flag it for acquisition consideration. If a property falls below performance thresholds, it can trigger recommendations for refinancing or divestment. Over time, this reduces emotional decision-making and replaces it with structured, data-driven execution.

Another critical component is continuous optimization. Unlike traditional portfolios that are reviewed periodically, autonomous systems operate in real time. Every variable—rent collection, expenses, market conditions, tenant behavior, and financing structures—is constantly analyzed. The system does not wait for monthly reports or quarterly reviews. Instead, it adjusts continuously to optimize performance. Rent adjustments, maintenance scheduling, and capital allocation decisions are all refined automatically based on evolving conditions.

AI also plays a central role in acquisition intelligence within autonomous systems. Instead of relying on manual deal sourcing or broker relationships, the system continuously scans markets for opportunities that meet predefined investment criteria. It evaluates cash flow potential, appreciation trends, financing feasibility, and risk exposure in real time. When a property aligns with strategic goals, it is automatically surfaced as a potential acquisition opportunity. This transforms deal flow from an active search process into a continuous, automated pipeline.

Financing within an autonomous system is also dynamically managed. Rather than treating loans as static obligations, the system continuously evaluates interest rates, equity positions, and capital efficiency across the portfolio. If better financing opportunities become available, the system identifies them and recommends action. Over time, this ensures that capital structure remains optimized without requiring manual monitoring or intervention.

Tenant management and property operations are also fully integrated into the autonomous structure. Tenant communication, lease management, maintenance coordination, and screening processes operate through automated workflows that adjust based on behavior patterns and portfolio conditions. This reduces friction, increases consistency, and ensures that operational performance remains stable even as the portfolio scales significantly.

Financial intelligence is another defining feature of autonomous real estate systems. Instead of reviewing financial performance after the fact, the system continuously evaluates cash flow, return on equity, and overall portfolio performance in real time. It identifies inefficiencies instantly and adjusts recommendations accordingly. Capital is continuously reallocated toward higher-performing assets, while underperforming assets are flagged for strategic action.

One of the most powerful outcomes of full autonomy is scalability without operational limits. In traditional real estate investing, growth is constrained by human capacity. More properties require more time, more management, and more oversight. In an autonomous system, scale becomes decoupled from effort. The system absorbs additional properties, markets, and transactions without increasing operational complexity. Each new asset simply becomes part of the existing intelligence framework.

Risk management is also embedded throughout the autonomous structure. The system continuously monitors financial exposure, market volatility, tenant behavior, and operational risks. When risk levels exceed acceptable thresholds, the system automatically initiates corrective strategies or alerts the investor. This proactive approach ensures that portfolio stability is maintained even during periods of market uncertainty.

Ultimately, Chapter 10 represents the completion of the transformation from investor to system architect. The goal is no longer to manage properties or even manage systems—it is to design systems that manage themselves. The investor's role shifts from operational involvement to strategic oversight, where the focus is on refining rules, adjusting parameters, and guiding long-term vision rather than executing daily tasks.

This is the final evolution of real estate investing: a fully autonomous, AI-powered wealth machine that operates continuously, adapts intelligently, and scales without friction.

### *The Day He Stopped Working In His Real Estate Business And Started Owning The System*

When Noah first started in real estate, he believed success meant control. He wanted to be involved in everything. He reviewed every deal personally, approved every expense, spoke to every tenant issue, and tracked every financial detail himself. In the beginning, that level of involvement gave him confidence. He felt connected to his investments and proud of how hands-on he was.

But as his portfolio grew, that control slowly turned into pressure.

Ten properties became twenty. Twenty became forty. And somewhere along the way, Noah stopped feeling like an investor and started feeling like an operator constantly reacting to problems.

He was always busy, but never ahead.

Every day brought new issues—maintenance requests, financing questions, tenant concerns, market fluctuations. No matter how organized he tried to be, the system always demanded more of his attention.

One night, after missing a refinancing opportunity that would have significantly improved his cash flow, Noah sat alone and realized something uncomfortable: he wasn't building wealth anymore—he was maintaining complexity.

That was the moment everything began to shift.

Not long after, Noah was introduced to an AI-driven autonomous real estate system built on integrated platforms like Buildium and AppFolio. At first, he assumed it was just another management tool. But what he discovered was something completely different.

It wasn't a tool.

It was a system that managed tools.

And more importantly, it made decisions.

At first, Noah watched cautiously as the system began organizing his portfolio. Tenant communications were streamlined. Maintenance workflows became automated. Financial reporting became real time instead of delayed. But the real change happened when the system began making recommendations.

It identified underperforming properties.

It flagged refinancing opportunities.

It highlighted tenants with risk patterns before issues occurred.

It even suggested acquisition opportunities in markets he had never considered.

Noah didn't know how to react at first. He had spent years believing that he had to make every decision himself. Trusting a system to make those decisions felt unnatural.

But he started small.

He followed one recommendation.

Then another.

Then another.

And something remarkable happened.

His portfolio started performing better.

More stable cash flow.

Fewer operational issues.

Improved financing structures.

Higher overall efficiency.

The system wasn't replacing him.

It was amplifying him. Months passed, and Noah began noticing something even more profound.

He was no longer managing daily operations.

He was reviewing outcomes.

The system handled execution.

He handled direction.

One evening, Noah opened his dashboard and realized something that made him pause.

Everything was running.

Properties were performing.

Tenants were being managed.

Finances were optimized.

Maintenance was being handled.

And he hadn't made a single operational decision that day.

That was the moment it fully clicked.

He wasn't running a real estate business anymore.

He was overseeing an autonomous system that ran it for him.

For years, he thought success meant being in control of everything.

Now he understood something completely different.

True scale wasn't control.

It was design.

And once the system was designed correctly, it didn't need him to run it.

It only needed him to guide it.

And for the first time in his life, Noah wasn't working inside his business.

He was finally free outside of it.

# Final Comments

*The Future Of Real Estate Is No Longer Manual*

At this point in your journey through AI-powered real estate investing, something fundamental should be clear. Real estate is no longer just a business of location, negotiation, and property ownership. It has evolved into something far more powerful and far more scalable—a system-based industry driven by data, automation, and artificial intelligence. The investors who thrive in the next decade will not be the ones who work the hardest manually, but the ones who design the strongest systems. Everything you have learned throughout this series leads to this final realization: success is no longer defined by how much you personally do, but by how intelligently your systems operate without you.

The traditional model of real estate investing was built on effort. Investors were expected to analyze deals manually, manage tenants directly, coordinate maintenance personally, track finances in spreadsheets, and scale through sheer workload capacity. That model has reached its limit. It does not scale efficiently, and it does not adapt quickly enough to modern market conditions. Artificial intelligence has permanently changed this equation. What once required teams, time, and constant attention can now be executed through integrated systems that operate continuously in the background.

Across this entire series, you have seen how AI transforms each layer of real estate investing. From deal sourcing and lead generation to property analysis, marketing, financing, portfolio management, tenant intelligence, scaling systems, and autonomous operations—every component of the real estate business has been redefined. Platforms such as Buildium and AppFolio are not just tools; they represent the foundation of a new operating structure where real estate portfolios function as intelligent ecosystems rather than manual operations.

The real shift that has taken place is not technological—it is mental. Most investors still think in terms of tasks: find deals, manage tenants, fix properties, collect rent, refinance loans. But AI forces a different way of thinking. It forces investors to think in terms of systems, workflows, and automation. Instead of asking "How do I do this task?", the new question becomes "How do I design a system that does this task forever without me?" That single shift in thinking is what separates small-scale investors from large-scale operators.

One of the most important lessons throughout this series is that complexity does not disappear as you scale—it multiplies.

Without systems, every new property adds more work, more decisions, and more potential for failure. But with AI-driven systems in place, complexity becomes manageable because it is absorbed by structure. The system becomes the filter between raw data and decision-making. It processes information, identifies patterns, and surfaces only what matters. This allows investors to operate at scale without becoming overwhelmed.

Another key insight is that real estate success is no longer linear. In the past, growth required proportional effort—more properties meant more work. Today, with AI integration, growth becomes exponential. Once systems are in place, each additional property does not add complexity; it strengthens the system. Data improves accuracy. Automation improves efficiency. Intelligence improves decision-making. The portfolio becomes more powerful as it grows, not more difficult to manage.

Throughout this series, we also explored how AI transforms financial performance. Traditional investing relies heavily on periodic reviews and backward-looking analysis. AI replaces this with continuous optimization. Cash flow, expenses, debt structures, and equity positions are no longer static numbers—they are dynamic variables that adjust in real time. This allows investors to make decisions based on current conditions rather than outdated reports. The result is faster execution, better capital allocation, and significantly improved portfolio performance over time. Tenant management and operational workflows have also been redefined. Instead of reacting to tenant issues as they arise, AI enables predictive and proactive management. Communication patterns, payment behaviors, and maintenance trends are analyzed continuously to identify risks before they escalate. This creates a more stable portfolio environment where problems are minimized and resolved earlier in their lifecycle. Stability, not chaos, becomes the default operating state of the business.

Perhaps the most important transformation discussed in this series is the transition from operator to architect. In traditional real estate investing, the investor is deeply involved in daily operations. In an AI-powered system, the investor becomes the designer of the system itself. Instead of executing tasks, they define rules, set parameters, and guide strategic direction. The system handles execution. This shift is what ultimately unlocks scale without burnout.

It is also important to understand that this transformation is not optional for the future—it is necessary. Markets are becoming faster, more competitive, and more data-driven. Investors who continue relying solely on manual methods will find themselves increasingly limited by time, inefficiency, and information gaps. Those who adopt AI-driven systems will operate with speed, clarity, and leverage that manual operators simply cannot match.

But perhaps the most powerful takeaway from this entire series is this: AI does not replace real estate investors—it amplifies them. It does not remove opportunity—it expands it. It does not eliminate control—it enhances it. When used correctly, AI becomes a force multiplier that allows investors to see more, decide faster, and scale further than ever before possible.

The future of real estate is not about working harder. It is about building systems that work intelligently without constant intervention. It is about designing portfolios that operate as ecosystems. It is about shifting from reactive management to proactive intelligence. And ultimately, it is about moving from being inside the business to standing above it as the architect of its entire structure.

If there is one final message to take from this series, it is this: the investors who win in the next era will not be the ones who own the most properties, but the ones who build the most intelligent systems. Real estate is no longer just about ownership. It is about orchestration.

And once you understand how to orchestrate systems instead of manually managing tasks, you are no longer limited by time, effort, or scale.

You are only limited by the intelligence of the system you choose to build.

www.ingramcontent.com/pod-product-compliance
Ingram Content Group UK Ltd.
Pitfield, Milton Keynes, MK11 3LW, UK
UKHW010012031026
15589UKWH00008B/1620

9 798295 885310